MANJIT BAWA

. . . in his own words

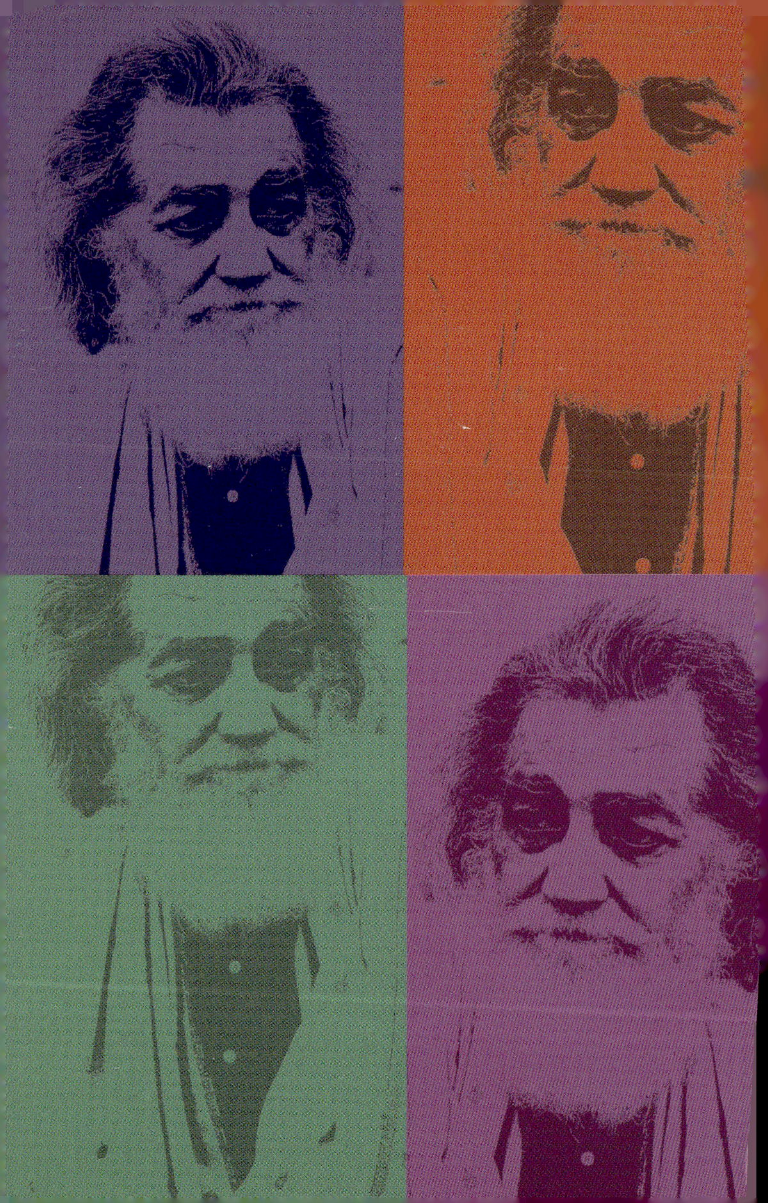

MANJIT BAWA

...in his own words

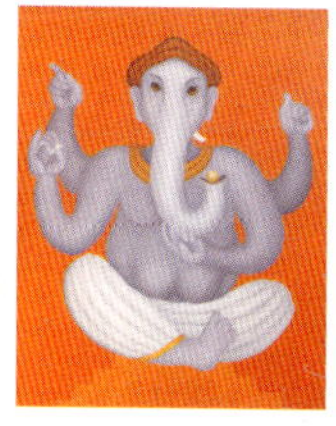

AS TOLD TO
Ina Puri

Lustre Press
Roli Books

Summer 2000. The Present

BUDAPEST, HUNGARY

I am allowing myself a few days off – these last three months have been especially busy, yet richly rewarding. I am told my exhibitions in New York, London and Amsterdam have been well received. And now, en route to Dalhousie and my empty canvas, before I start cleaning my brushes or mixing my colours, I am giving myself these few days to reminisce, to poke and prod into the indistinct canvases of my early days. I have not explored for a long while. Where should I begin?

Time is running out . . . .

'Time is running out.' I had thought the same then too and the sequence of events prompting the thought comes slowly into sharper focus before my eyes.

The lazy blue-grey smoke spiralling upwards from the *chula* (stove) as Bijee patiently prepares our meagre evening meal. At some distance

Papaji is distributing his home remedy in little *puriyas* (packets) to his patients who swear that they are so benefited by Papaji's medicine, prepared painstakingly from herbs and spices by my mother, that they will never trust another doctor in their life! Grimly I view the domestic routine, our modest quarters, our little home. Soon my elder brothers will return from work, my sister from her sewing class and I will have to sacrifice my private hour with Papaji, sitting on his large comfortable lap and nestling against his luxuriant beard. A magical hour in enchanted lands brimming over with gods and heroes. It is our time together and my eyes smart with tears to see the hand of the clock

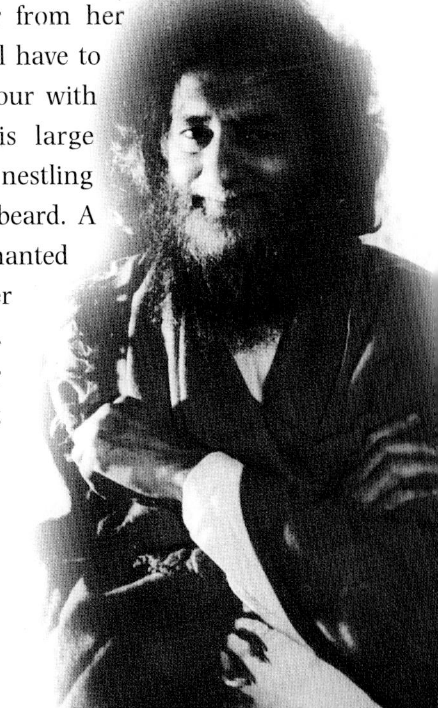

Times moves on . . . Manjit Bawa.

move relentlessly forward. Three years of age, I am the seventh of eight children in a family which has recently moved to Delhi from Dhuri, now on the wrong side of the Punjab, where I was born, strangely enough, in a cowshed!

Back in Dhuri we were respected land-owners, a far cry from our humble situation in Delhi. In order to keep the family clothed and fed, my elder brothers have to take up jobs at the cost of their education. Our financial crisis is also the result of my father's unwise trust in his friend-cum-partner, who has cold-heartedly swindled him of all the family's savings. But I am secure in the warmth of my parents' affection.

The city of Delhi is like one of Daniel's watercolours – so vividly green and beautiful. It is this vividness in colours all around me which will later lay its stamp on my art. Meanwhile, the scars of Partition are subjects the family elders whisper furtively about. I am too young and too involved in my carefree pursuits to be affected by its horrors. In the late '40s and early '50s, I spend my time playing truant from school and as

I grow older I set off on my cycle to explore, in ever-increasing circles, the joys of this old city.

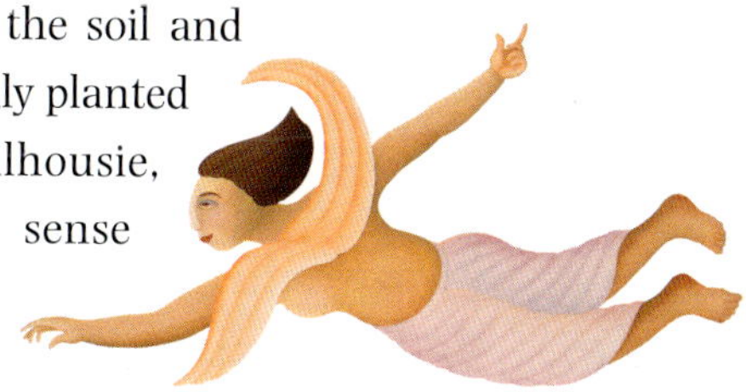

Close to home, Connaught Place is a favourite haunt – I love to gaze at the great flocks of parrots that descend on the lawns in an emerald cloud of feathers. The memory of parting the long grass in spring, to discover the first violets . . . remains with me 50 years later (much as my love for the soil and the seeds I have fruitfully planted in my garden in Dalhousie, redelivers the same sense of wonder). And the reckless surge of excitement while surreptitiously leading friends to neighbourhood orchards to gorge on mangoes, *jamuns* (blackberries) or guavas! What delight! Despite every attempt to keep a strict vigil over me, I somehow manage to escape – to try and discover more of the city's natural pleasures, its innumerable sights and sounds. Ancient mosques, monuments and *quillas* (forts) lie strewn across Old Delhi; street life fascinates me and I fill up my notebooks with sketches of street scenes – horse-drawn carriages, veiled women, snake charmers and cows indolently lazing in the middle of crowded roads.

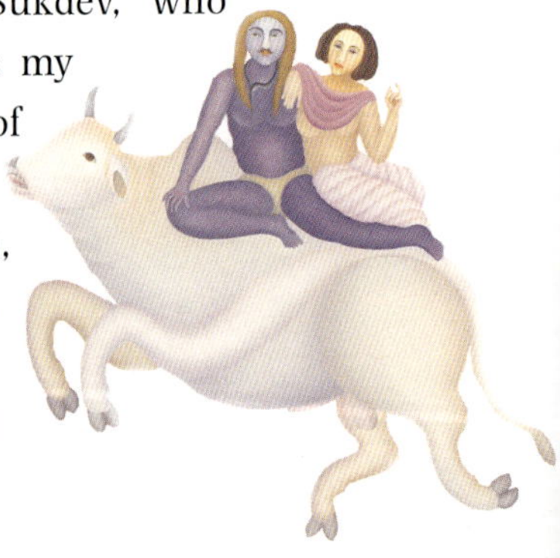

I also love sketching the profiles of Sardar Kulwant Singh and Bibi Satyabati Kaur – my parents; they personify, to my young heart, the qualities of pride and dignity. My bonding with both my parents remains as I grow up and becomes somewhat of a concern to my brothers who seek to curb my exuberance and escapades with sound thrashings. I seriously consider school to be a drain on my time and concentration so I stay away (to the great annoyance of my elder brothers, especially Manmohan and Sukdev, who consider themselves my guardians). Both of them punish and cajole me in turn, till we finally reach a state of truce. I promise to attend class in exchange for permission to go on cycle expeditions during school vacations. I am quickly learning the art of negotiation!

This is a great contract and very soon, accompanied by Ranjan Sen and Nilmani, I cycle off to Rajasthan, Uttar Pradesh, Madhya Pradesh, Jammu and Kashmir, Himachal Pradesh and even to Mumbai in distant Maharashtra. Of course these are tough journeys but I love the sense of adventure and the width and variety of all I see and experience. Looking back I feel this was the beginning of what I am today – a restless traveller in love with the world. Carrying a backpack and surviving in the wilderness with meagre provisions are tests that I have frequently set for myself. And there has never been any room for compromise. All through my travels, I have sketched the essence of spellbinding landscapes and monuments, which have later indirectly formed my art. Sketching and painting was what I did instinctively but it never occurred to me, as a youth, that art could be a serious career option.

There were no 'painters' in my parents' generation or family. Yet I knew, in a corner of myself, that art was my very life and soul.

School ends and now career prospects are being discussed – Manmohan broaches this sensitive subject. Taking up my cause he says he will take complete charge of my education and with his support, I join the Delhi Art College. The year I begin my formal training is 1958; Nehru's tryst with destiny is alive and India is awash with hope and optimism. At this time I have the good fortune to meet the erudite scholar and gifted painter, Abani Sen, who agrees to act as my guide through the maze: which is the art world. An austere yet gentle person, Abani Sen opens my eyes to the contemporary art scene in India and Europe. Reverentially we pore over hefty tomes to minutely examine and discuss the works of Klee, Miro, Van Gogh, Rembrandt, Cezanne, El Greco, and so many more.

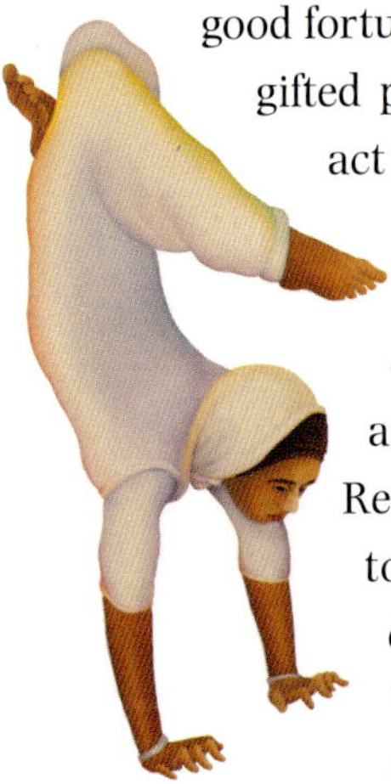

In college, we are shown the preparatory drawings of Michelangelo – the final acts of which are immortalised in the Sistine Chapel. The works of early Renaissance painters, Rubens, Raphaël, continue to hold sway many centuries after their death. Our practical classes involve reproducing these great European masters, much against my personal wishes. Ideas torment me and thoughts of what I want to achieve hinder my attentiveness in class and I am often rebuked for my absent-mindedness. Truth is, I desperately long to express myself but am unsure of the response this will evoke.

Our faculty boasts of some really well-known names in the art circle – Biren Dé, Somnath Hore, B. Sanyal and Sailoz Mukherjee (fashionably bohemian, he shocks and amuses us with his unconventional sartorial excesses). It is in Art College too that we see the works of Rabindranath Tagore, Ram Kinkar Baij and Binode Bihari Mukherjee. I enjoy their works tremendously but am careful to steer away from influences.

It is with a lot of financial difficulty that I

continue my studies at Art College and I am eager to make the most of it. I never shirk classes and devote my entire energy and focus to the curriculum but am never sure or comfortable with the end towards which these means are taking me. I know I have to be an artist, yet it should only be on my terms. To help sort out my state of confusion I turn to my professor, Rajesh Mehra. And in his quiet way, it is Rajesh Mehra who helps me resolve my artistic afflictions. He gives me support, stability and self-belief.

Drawing was always my greatest strength and I loved the process so much that my hands always seemed to move of their own accord across sketch pads leaving flowing lines in their wake. But with painting I often feel defeated – the prevalent

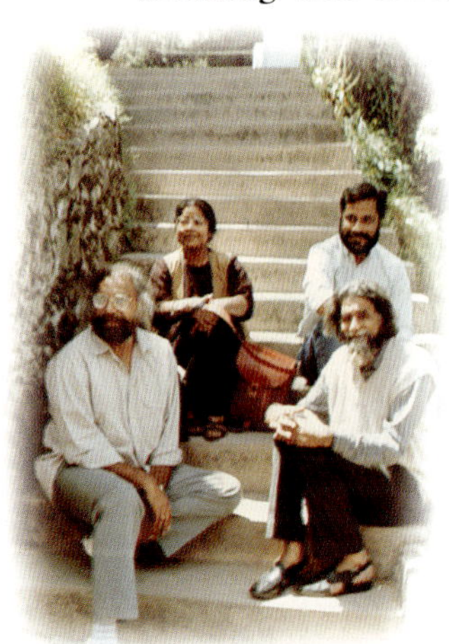

Manjit Bawa with Paramjit Singh and Arpita Singh.

use of dull, fashionably 'European' colours – blue, grey, beige – are foreign to my imagination or vocabulary. Childhood impressions of fleeting russet sunsets remain forever inside my mind's eye; like the vibrant pinks, greens, yellows, purples and other colours that paint our Indian landscape in bold shades, I seek to make them an integral part of my language. I read Matisse's autobiography, where he says he has dreamed, from his earliest years, of the radiant light and colour he finally achieves towards the end of his life in the stained-glass windows of the chapel in Venice in 1952: 'It is the whole of me . . . everything that was best in me as a child'. Matisse's entire life is a flight towards light to escape the gloomy, barren landscape of Bohain. In my case, I have walked through green paddy fields from childhood and bathed in the blue waters of the Beas; I have seen the celebration of colour in Holi and in the *phulkari* shawls being woven – I have been born to brightness and colour; to pretend they do not exist is difficult.

At about this time, I receive a marvellous

invitation – to join David Letchman, an intrepid traveller, on his road journey from Delhi to London. It is the early '60s and I have just completed college, which makes the timing perfect. Getting my family to say Yes is not easy; but once I get their blessings, I jump into this new adventure with abandon. In many ways, this is a turning point in my life, offering me the opportunity to taste first-hand, strange and wonderful cultures. The romance of driving through the deserts, mountains and towns of Afghanisthan, Turkey, Greece, Italy, France is unforgettable. Also my first taste of wine and the freedom which comes from acquiring a few points of reference to understand the wider world.

Once we reach England, I decide to try for a scholarship and continue studying. For the next eight years I remain in London simultaneously studying and teaching and on the way picking up a degree in printmaking. Ironically, I become such an expert at printing that for a while all my time is taken up with printing orders! But this is not what I have set out to achieve. So gradually, working just enough to earn a living, I spend all my waking hours painting, gradually developing my craft. In 1968 my responsibilities increase as I marry Sharda, my favourite sister Darshan's friend. Being a musician herself, she is supportive and understanding. When I want to return to India, she agrees without demur and we come back home to Delhi.

It is all so different now or maybe I have changed – but the city of my childhood is a busy metropolis now and quite alien. I am aware that by this time, my work has attained a certain distinctive style and standard. My experiments with colour are now complemented by a very personal play with limbs and space. Looking back I realise the greatest influence here is the exercise games I constantly invent for my young son, Ravi who can neither hear nor

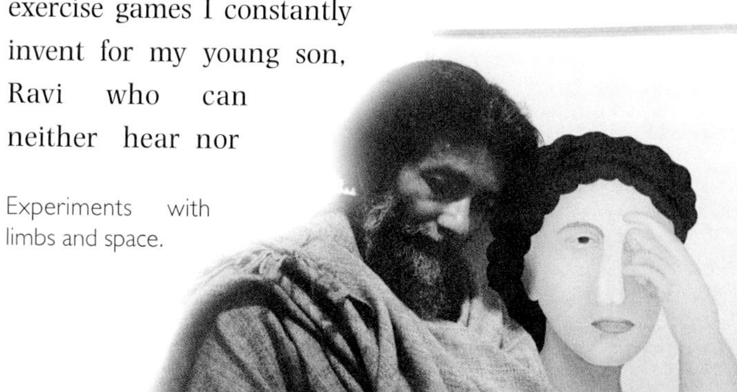

Experiments with limbs and space.

speak! It is the gutsy Swaminathan, who first writes extensively about me and then organises my show. I am 38 years old and have never till now, seriously bothered to think of actually selling my paintings. The exhibition – my first serious showing – is a success, and I have had no painting of mine since to call my own!

Poverty, religious intolerance and ethnic violence are a constant source of anguish to me. I often relive the nightmarish hours of the Delhi riots in 1984 when innocent Sikhs were brutally butchered for no fault of their own. That was a time when I became very busy trying in my own small way to bring a split city together again, a time when my interest in and belief in Sufism deepened and became one of the central tenets of my being. The cause of ahimsa and peaceful co-existence of all beings finds itself reflected in my work. Though I have always reacted practically to crises rather than run to my easel, Picasso's 'Guernica' is to me the last word in protest – no armed riots can ever achieve what this astonishing painting has done . . . .

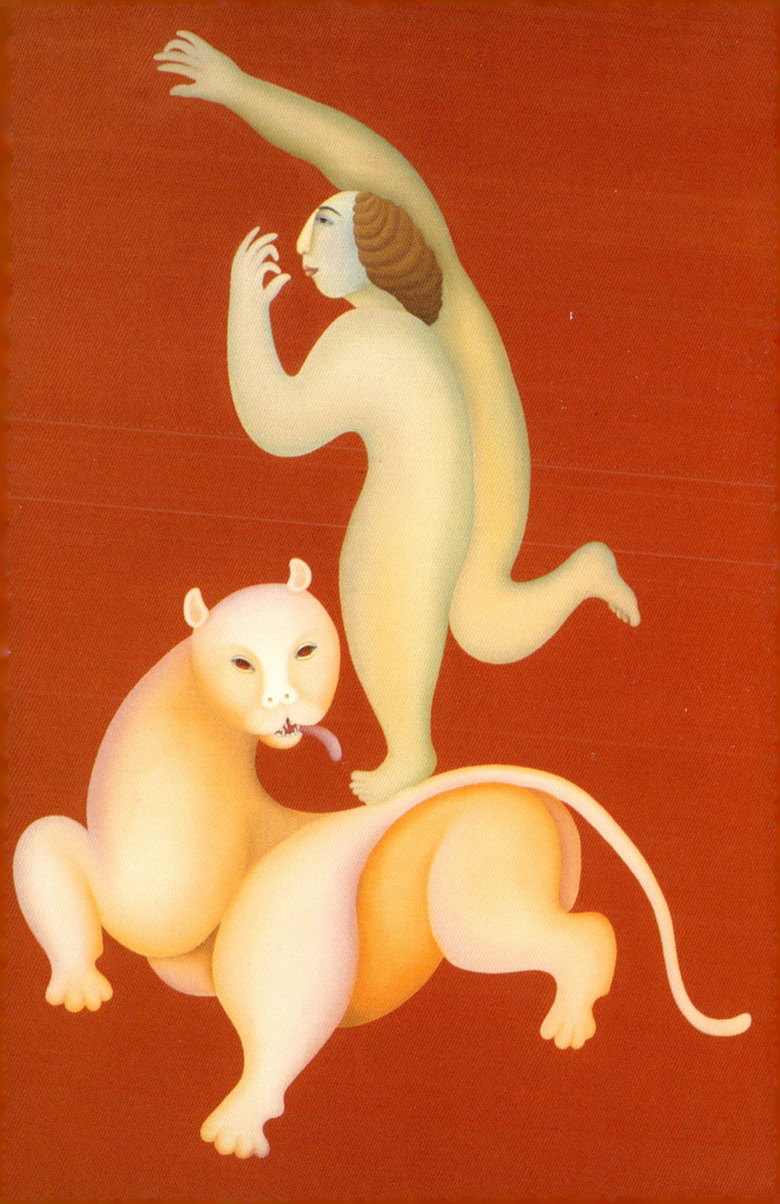

■ Untitled

88" x 60", oil on canvas, 1995

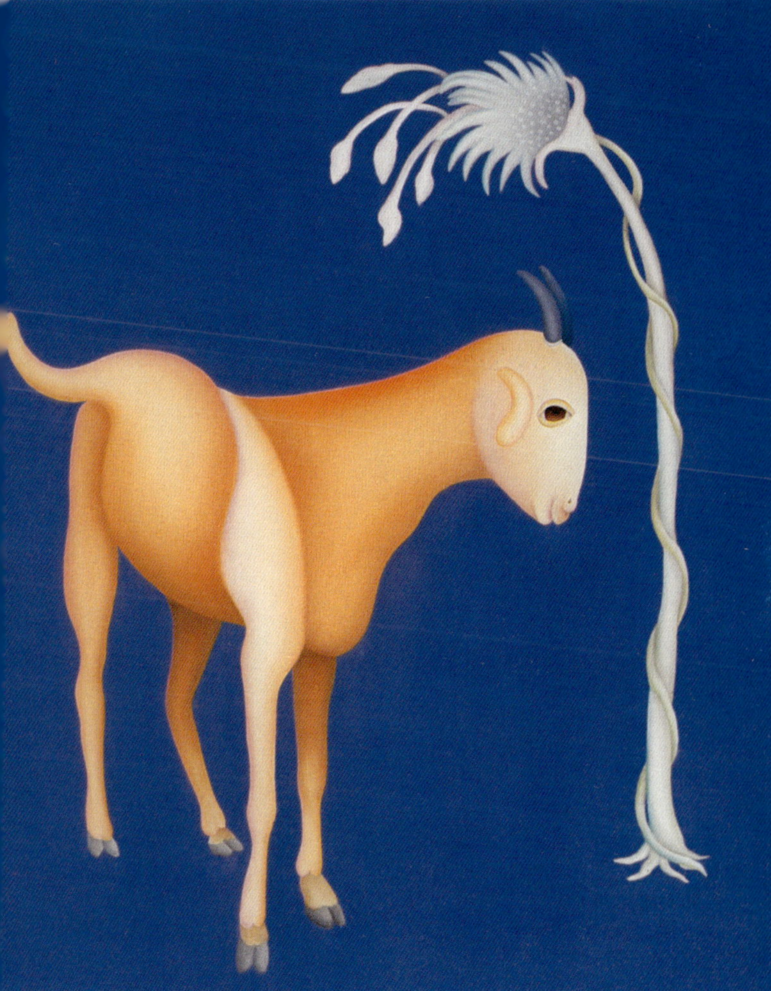

■ Untitled

46" x 36", oil on canvas, 1994

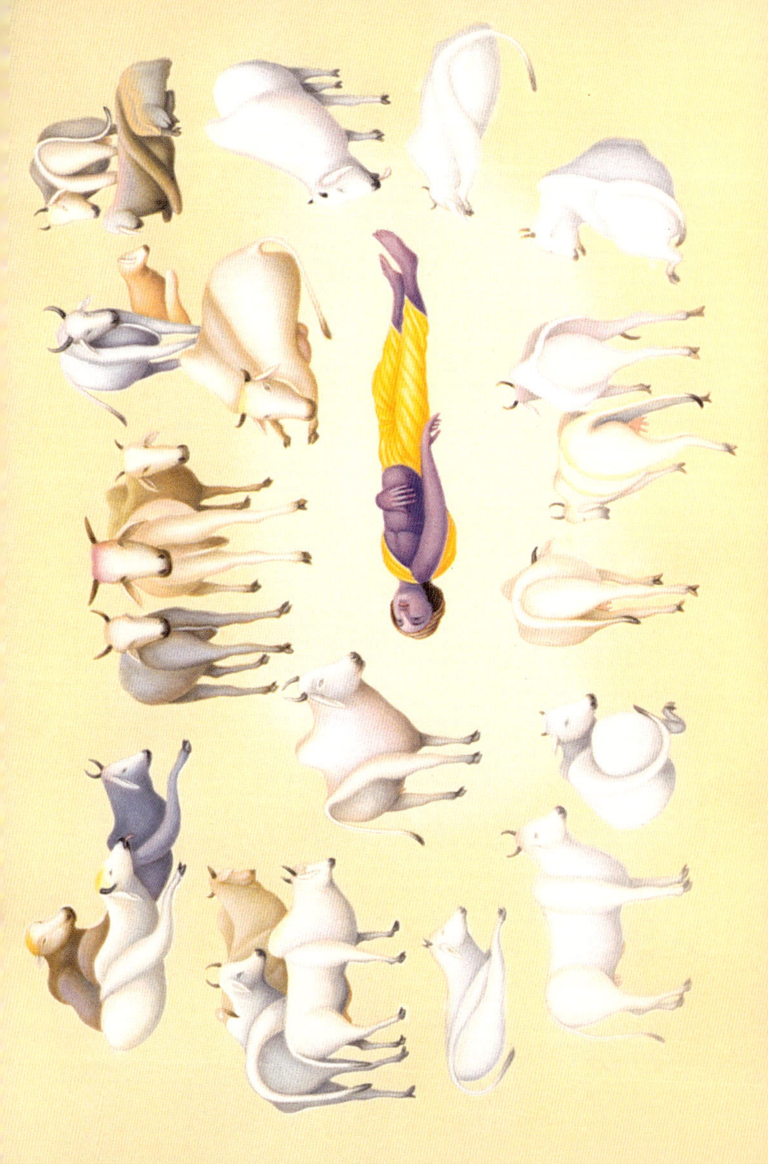

■ Death of Krishna

70" x 95", oil on canvas, 1993

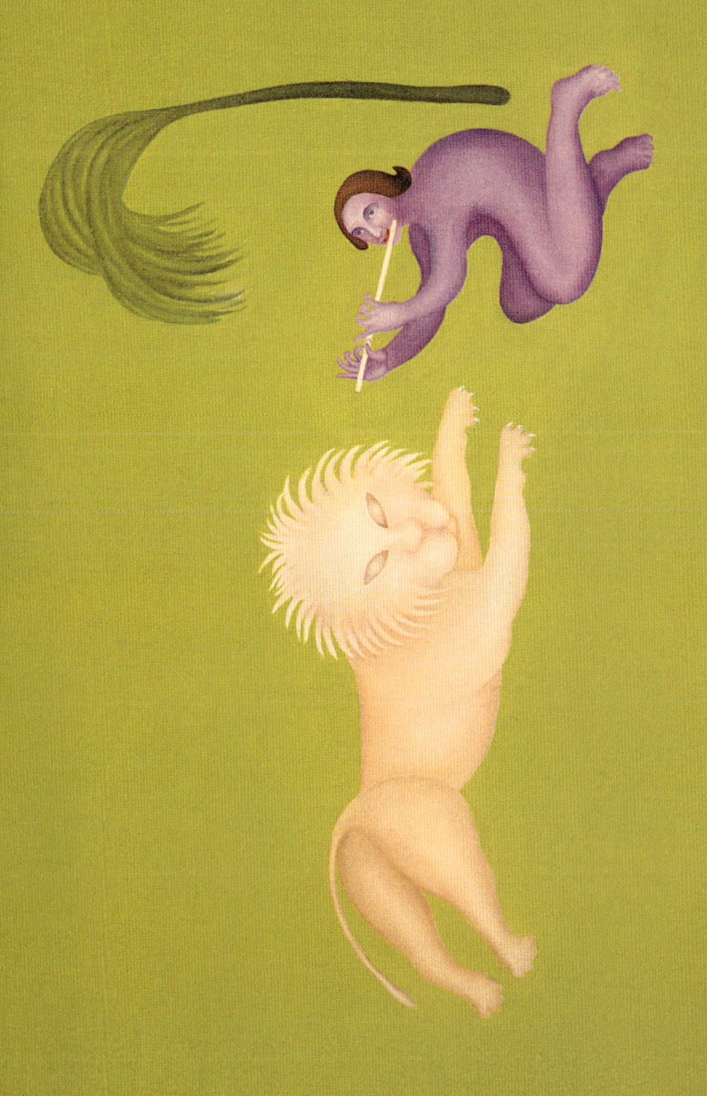

■ Untitled

45" x 32", oil on canvas, 1981

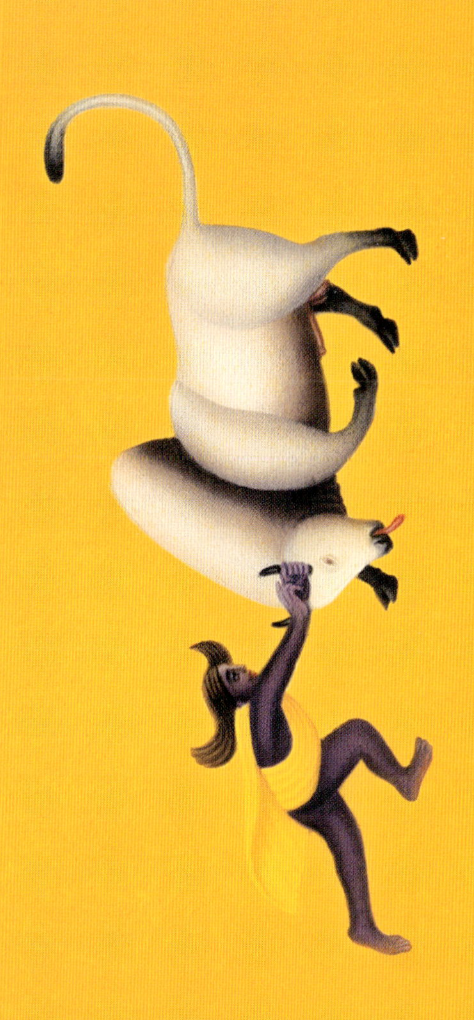

■ Miniature

7" x 11", oil on canvas, 1995

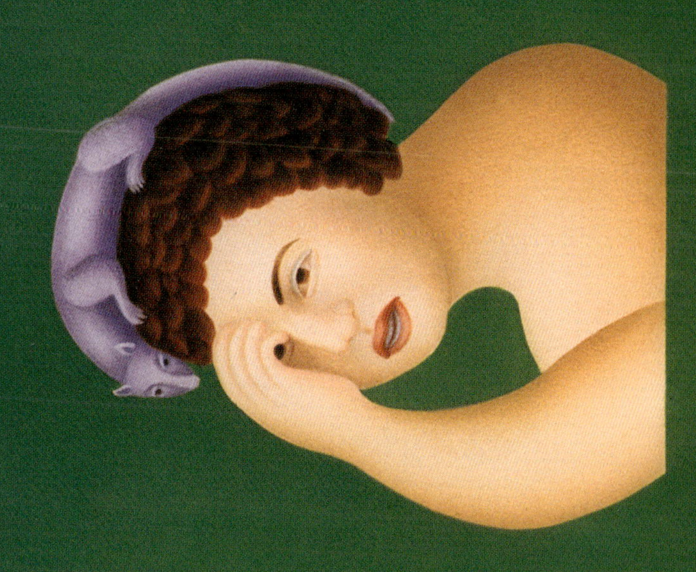

■ Miniature series

4" x 6", oil on canvas, 1992

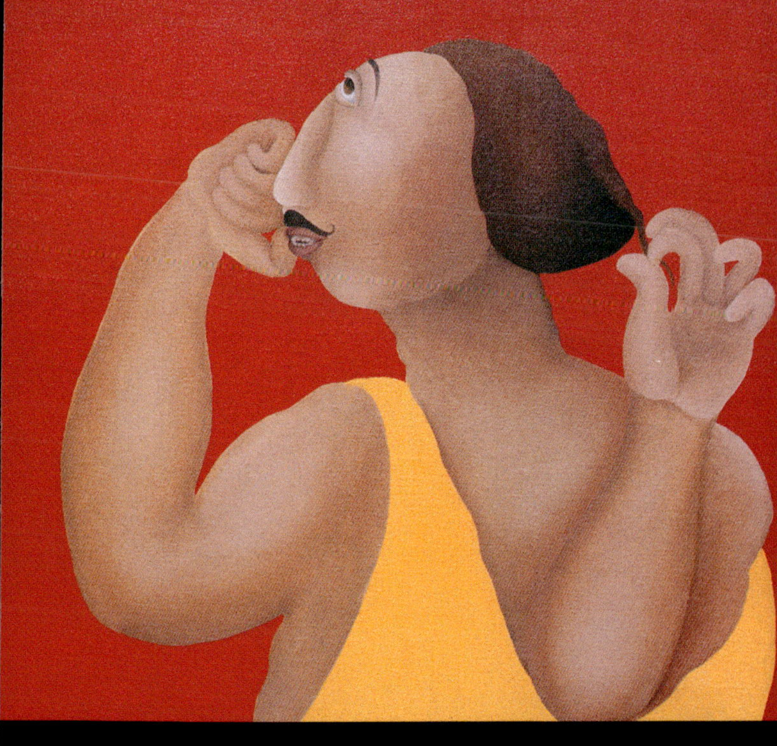

■ Untitled

22" x 24", oil on canvas, 1983

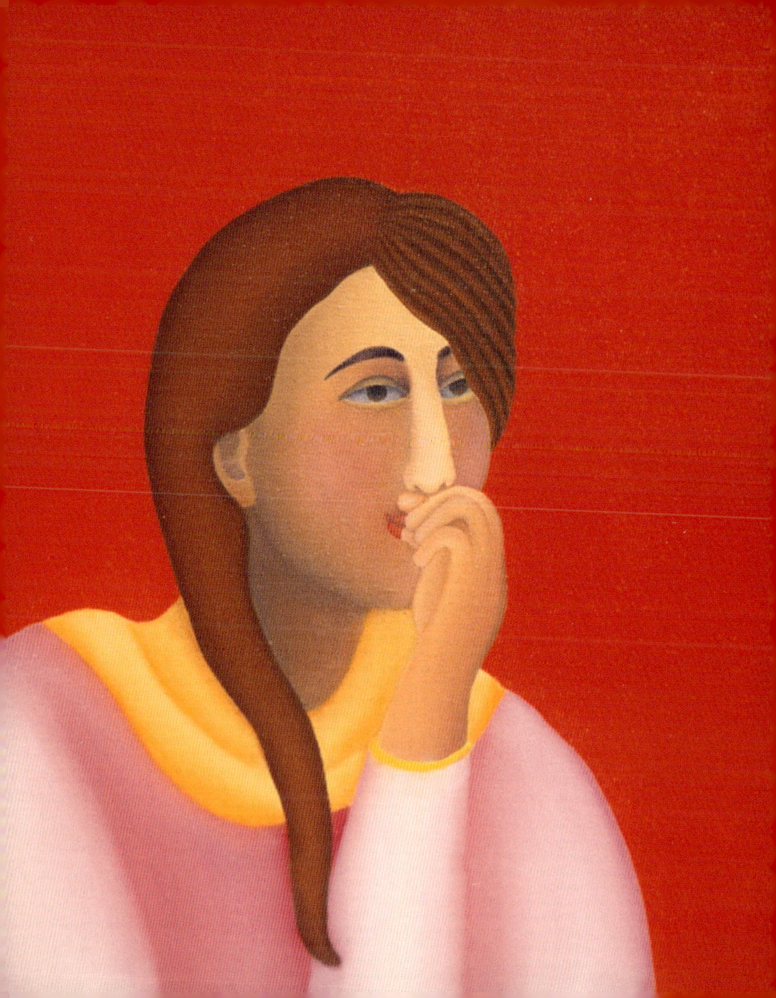

■ Woman in pink

22" x 26", oil on canvas, 1996-97

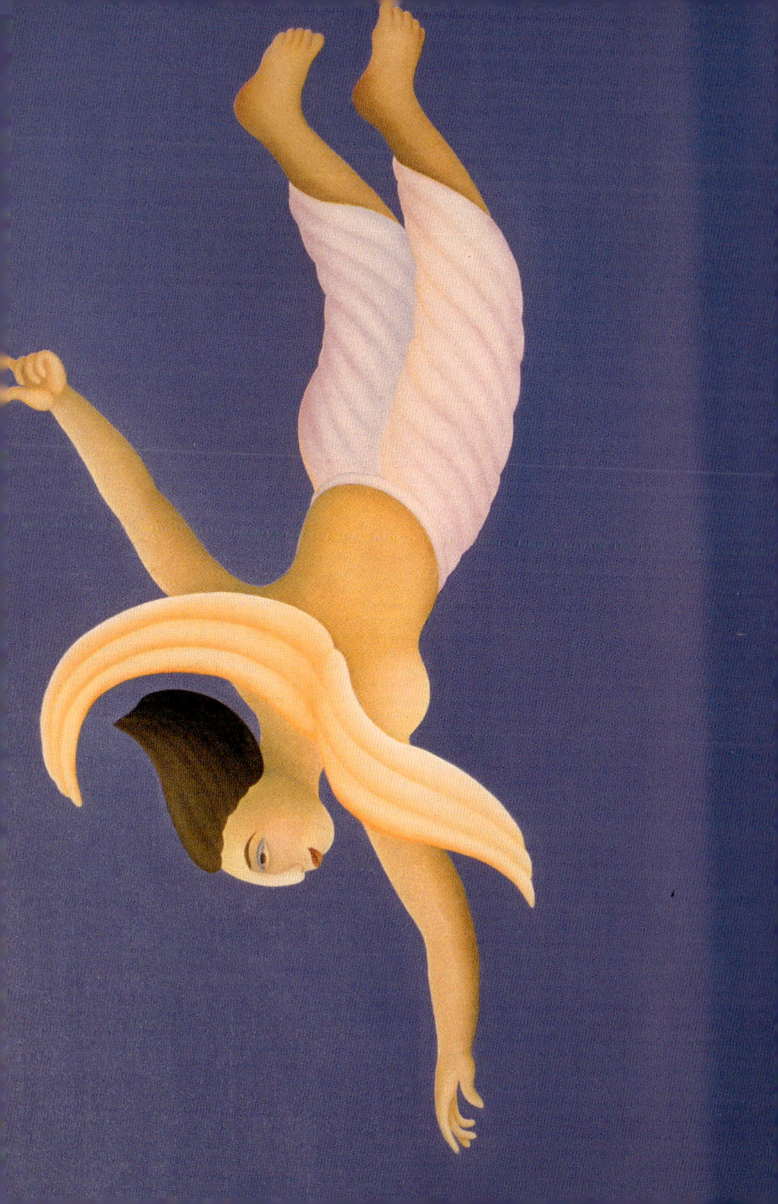

■ Untitled

64" x 42", oil on canvas, 1996

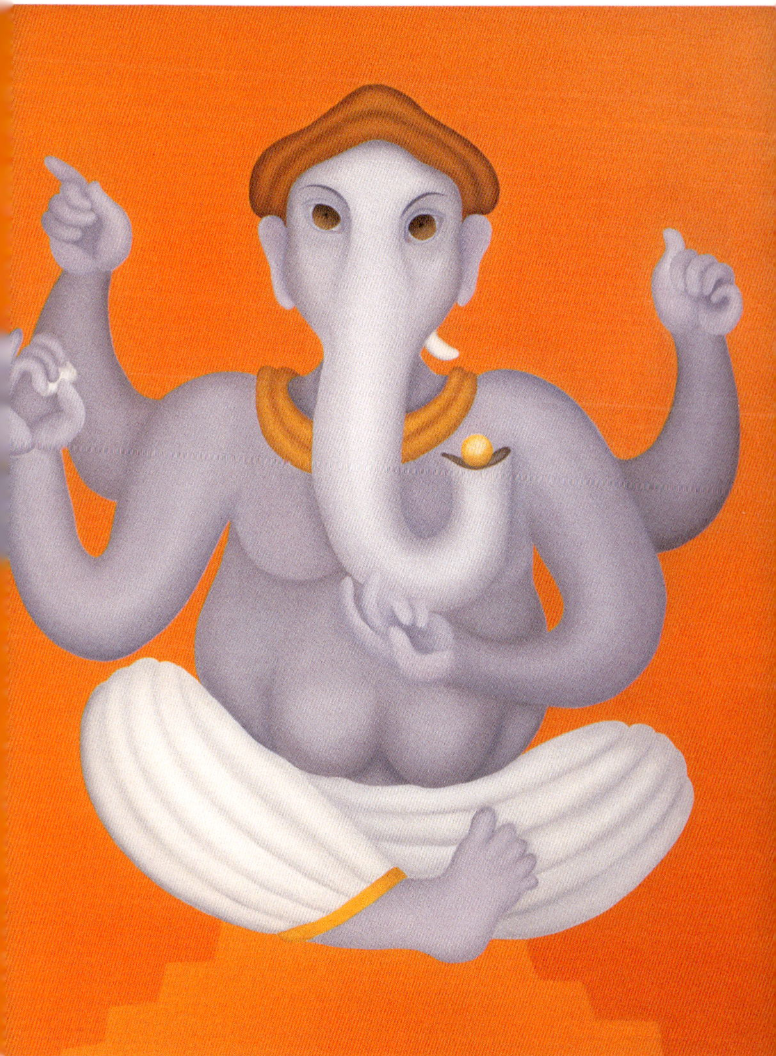

■ Untitled

60" x 48", oil on canvas, 1982

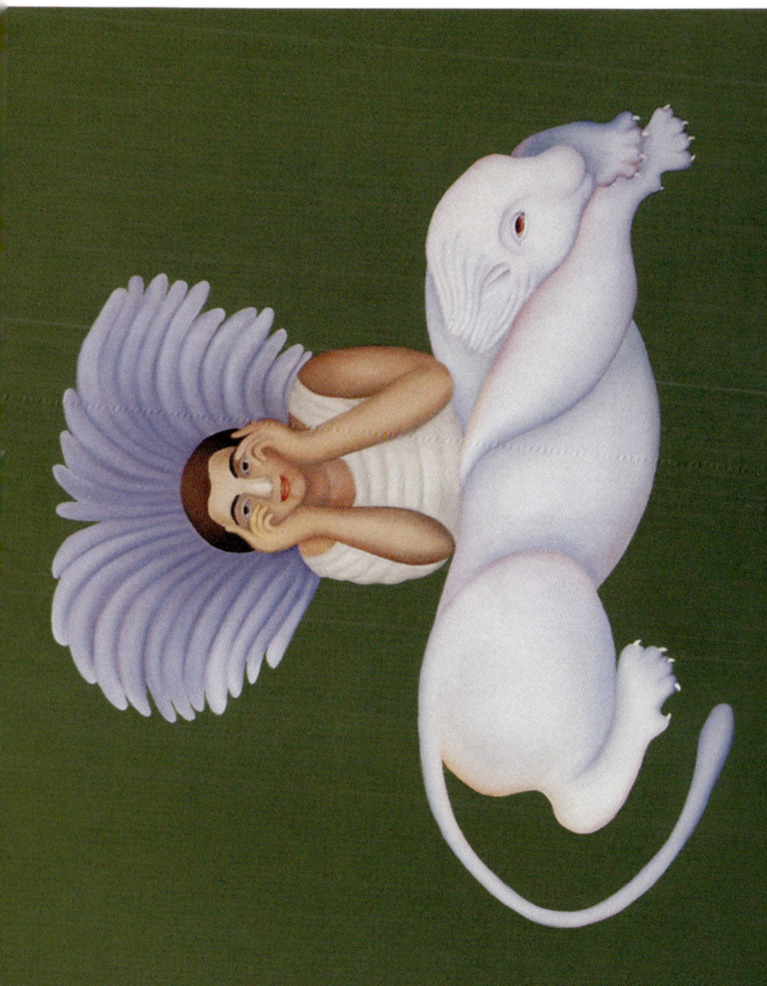

■ Untitled

54" x 43", oil on canvas, 1985

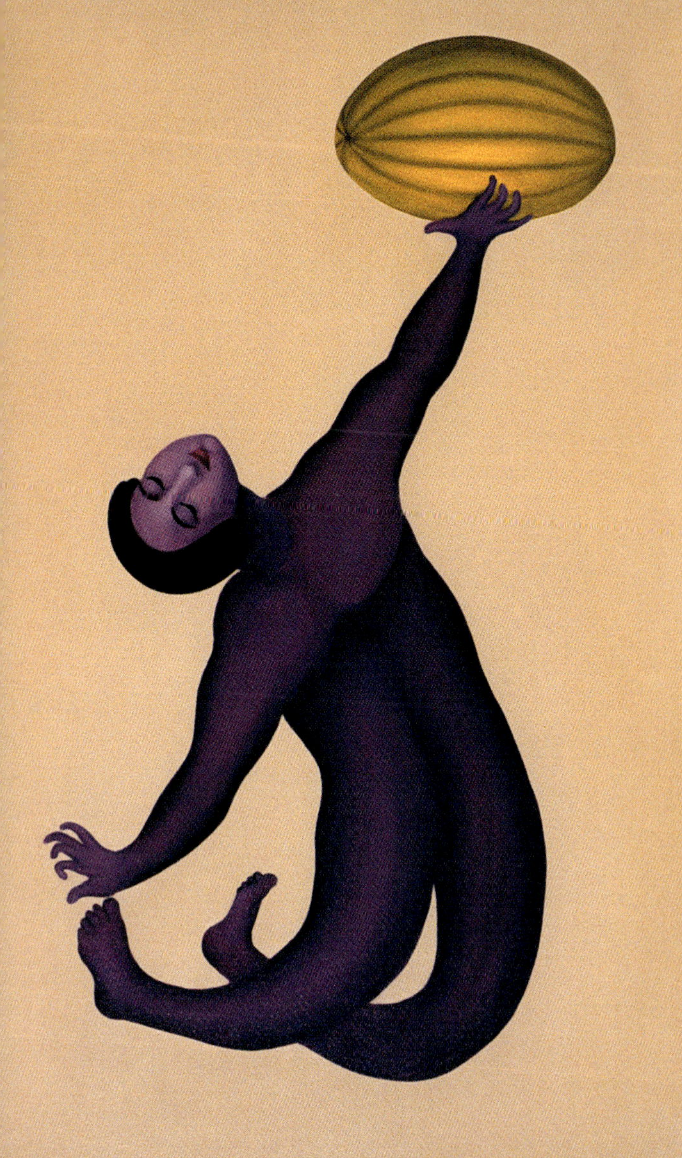

■ Krishna

44" x 32", oil on canvas, 1985

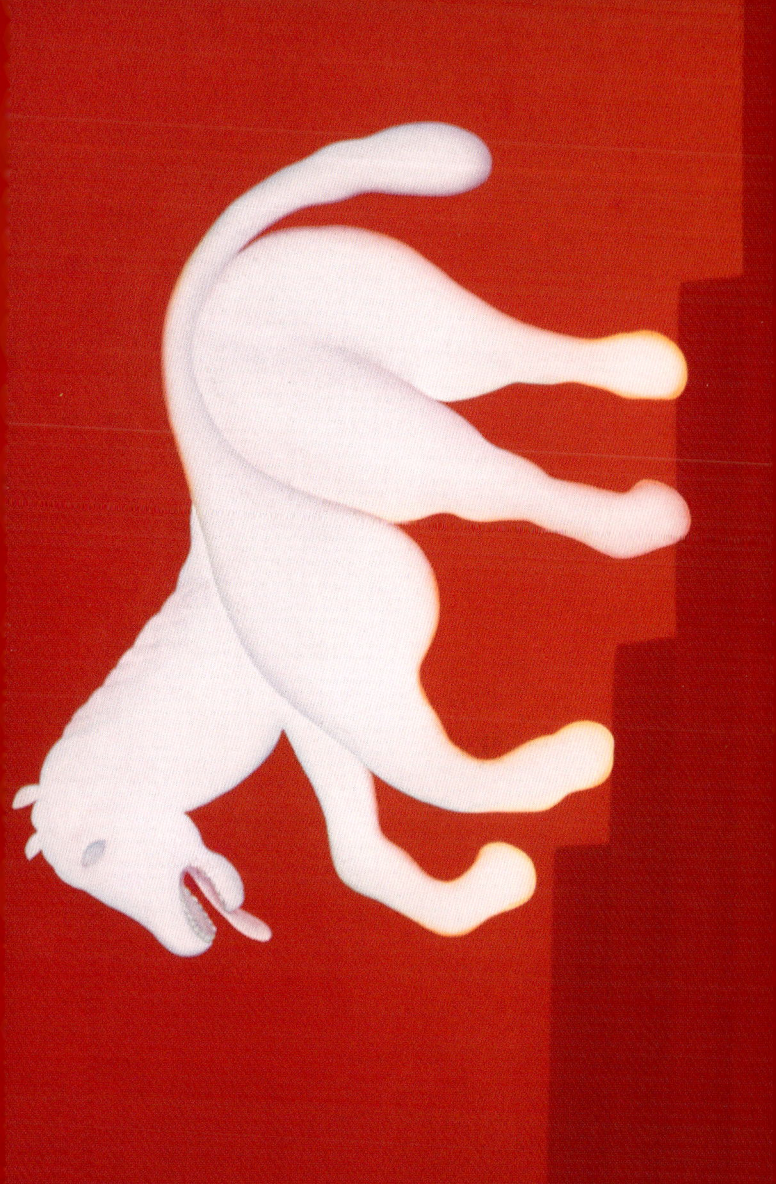

■ A horse who is white

136 cm x 172 cm, oil on canvas, 1979

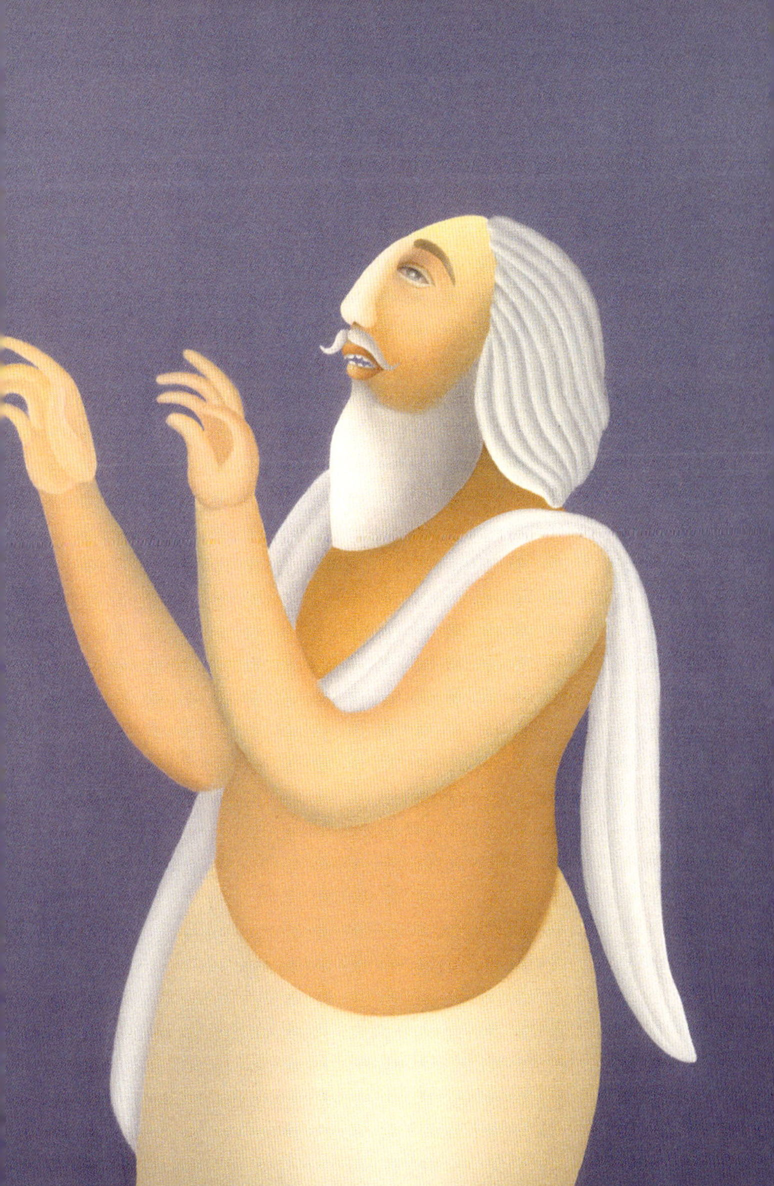

■ Untitled

35" x 41", oil on canvas, 1999

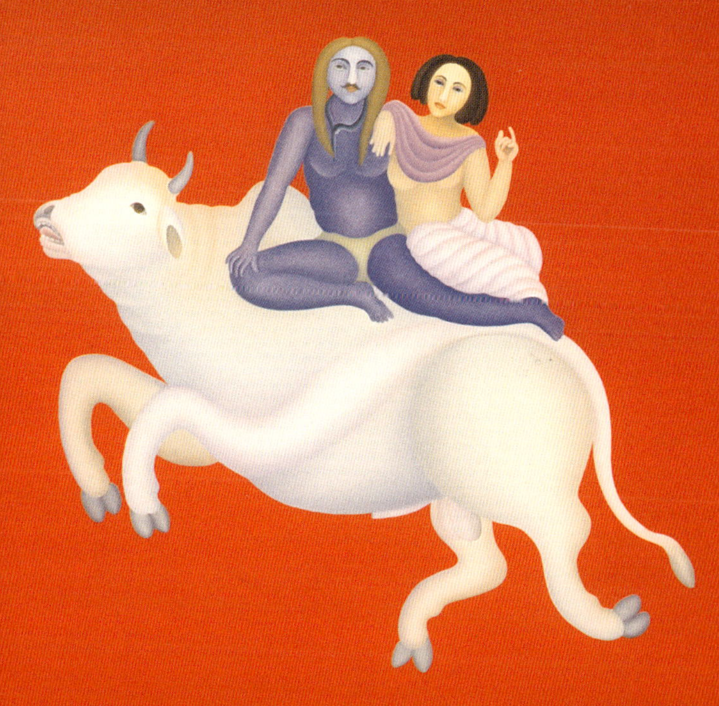

■ Untitled

66" x 60", oil on canvas, 2000

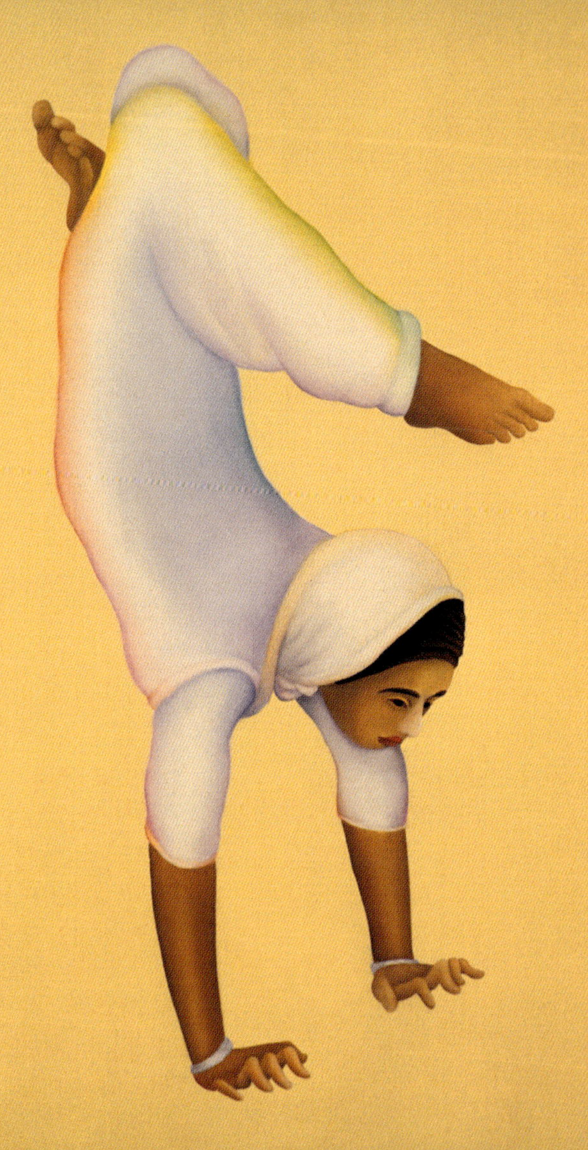

■ Untitled

46" x 43", oil on canvas, 1993

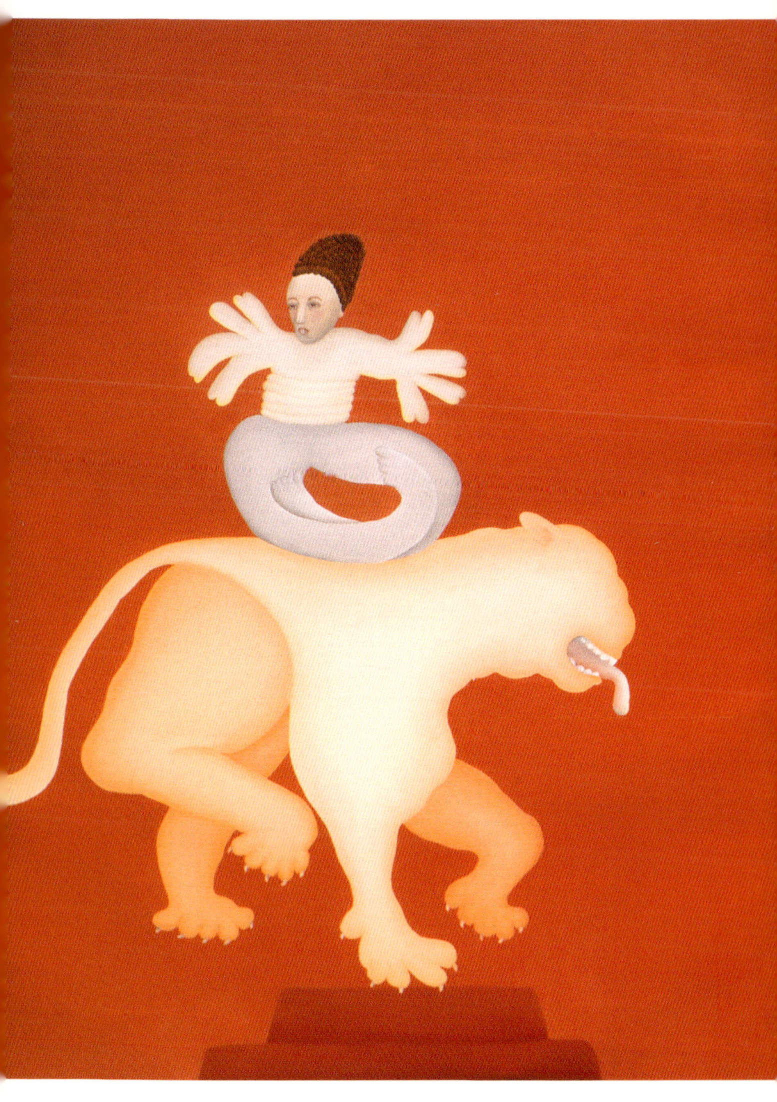

■ Untitled

68" x 52", oil on canvas, 1982

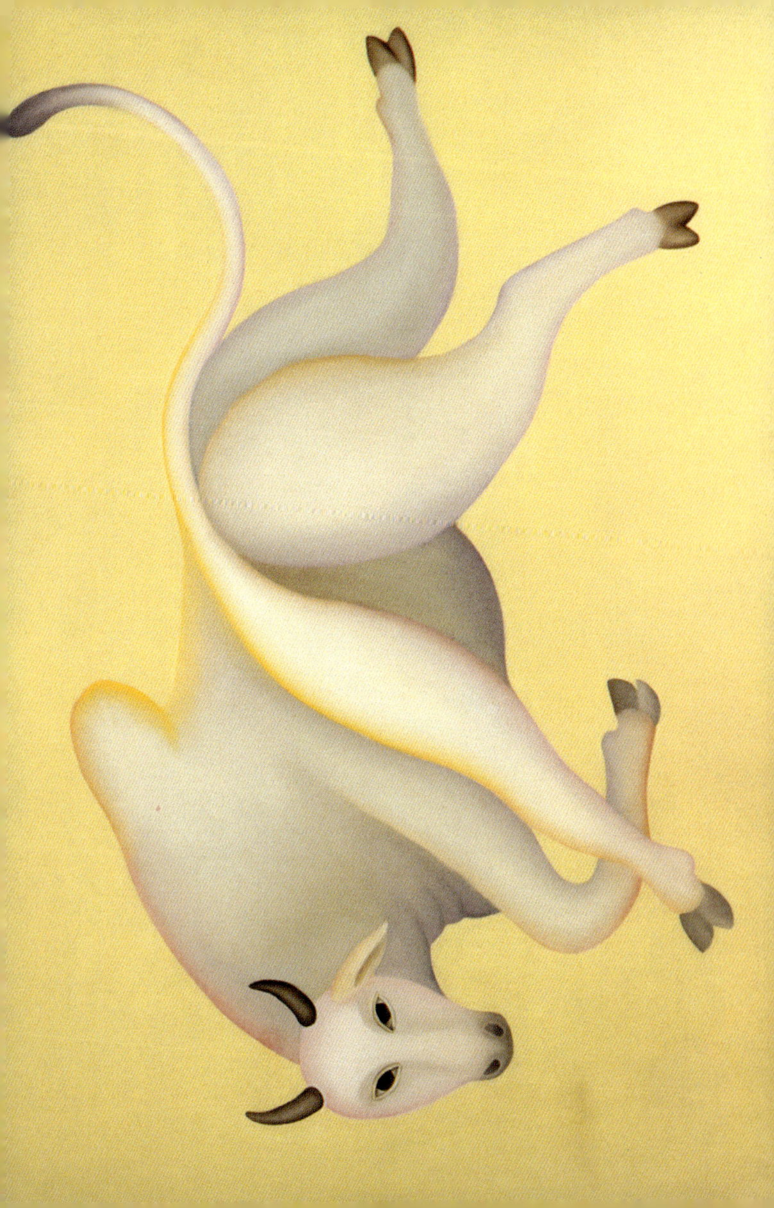

■ Untitled

62" x 45", oil on canvas, 1992

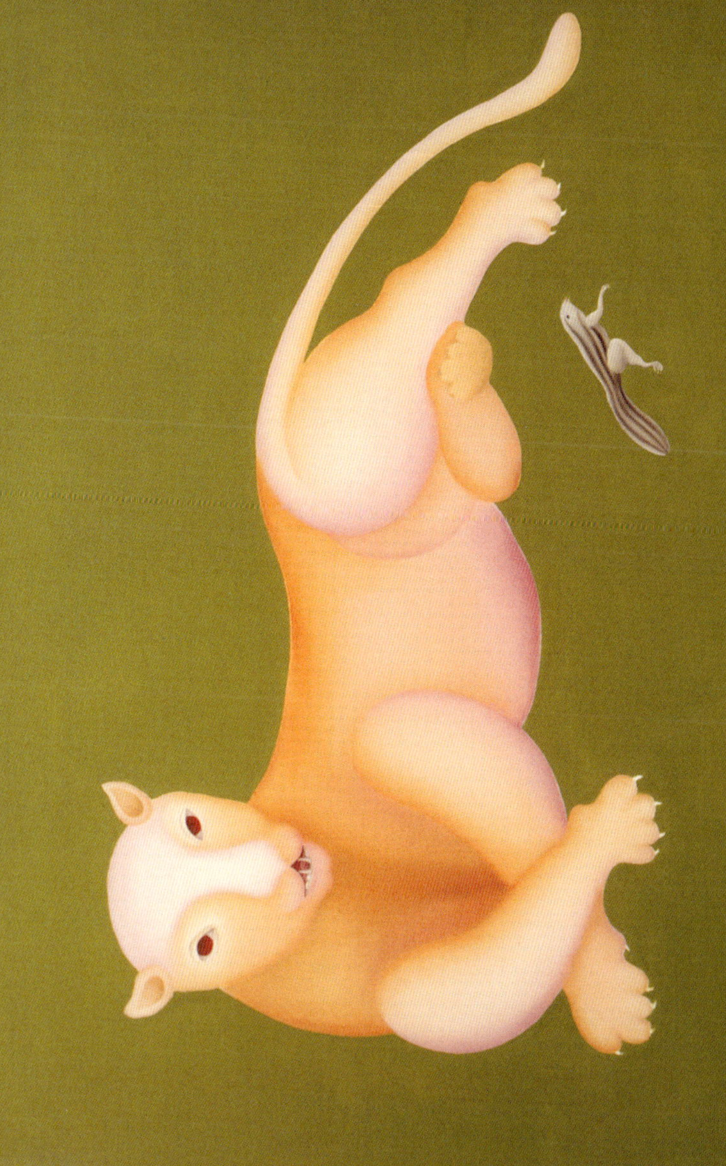

■ Lion with a green background

40" x 55", oil on canvas, 1998

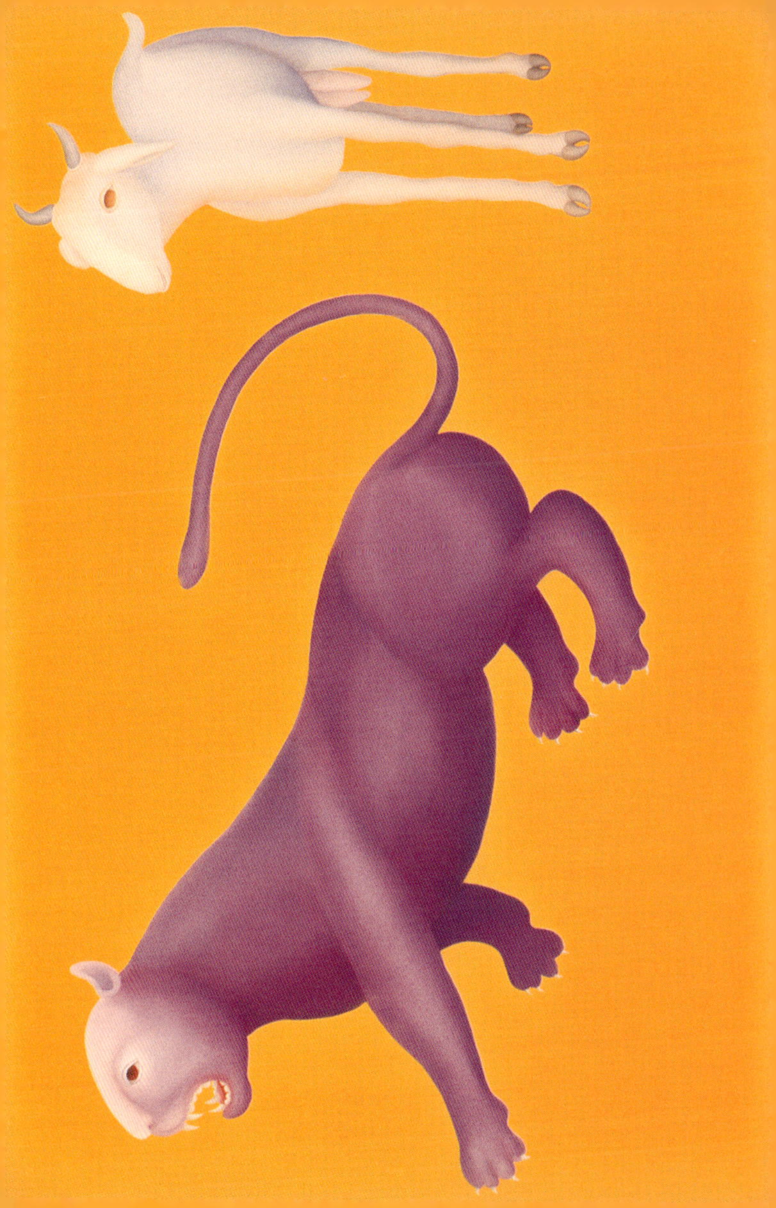

■ Untitled

80" x 48", oil on canvas, 1998

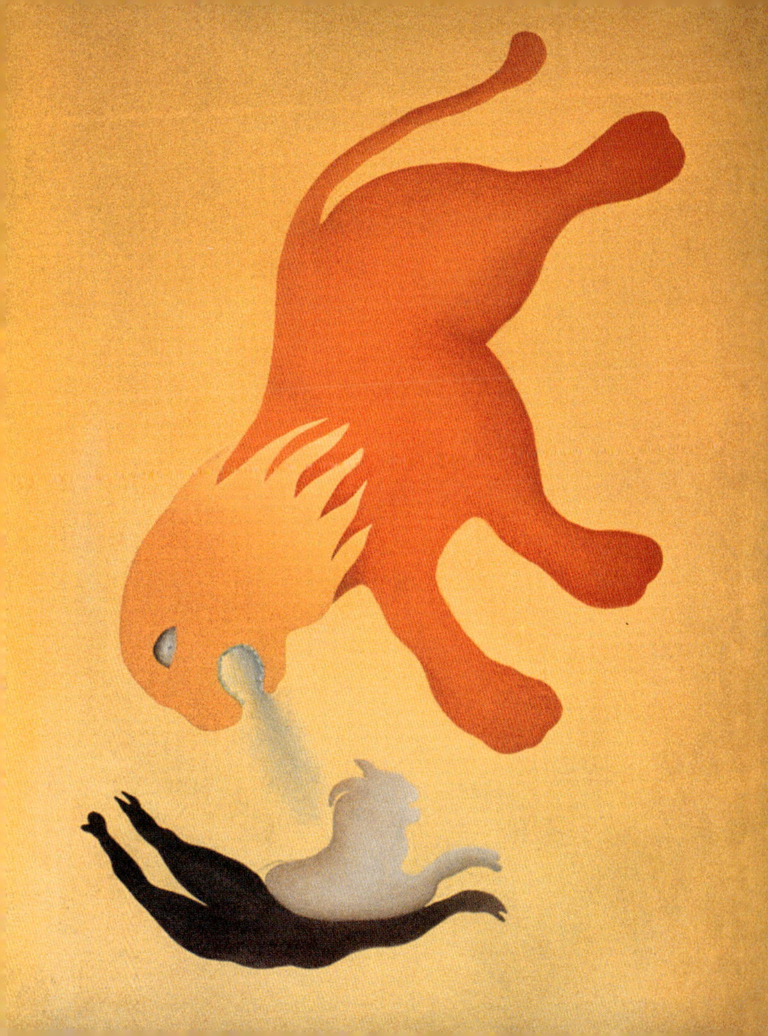

■ Untitled

42" x 36", oil on canvas, 1979

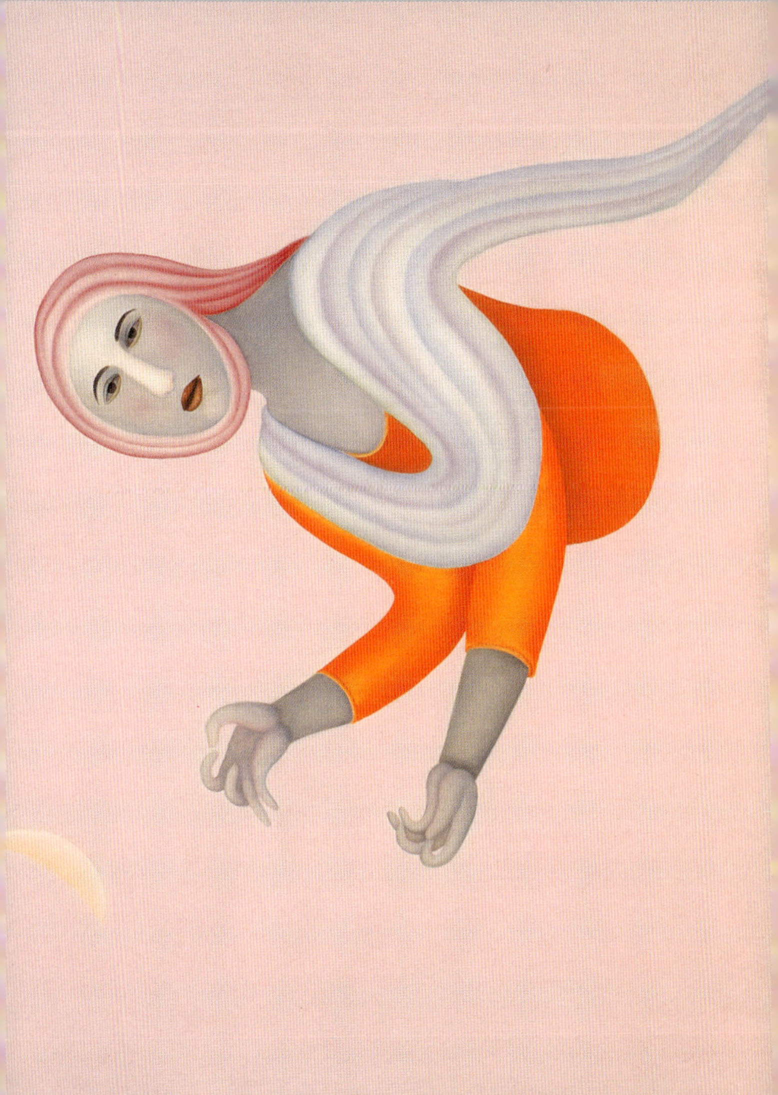

■ Woman with arms stretched

35" x 46", oil on canvas, 1994

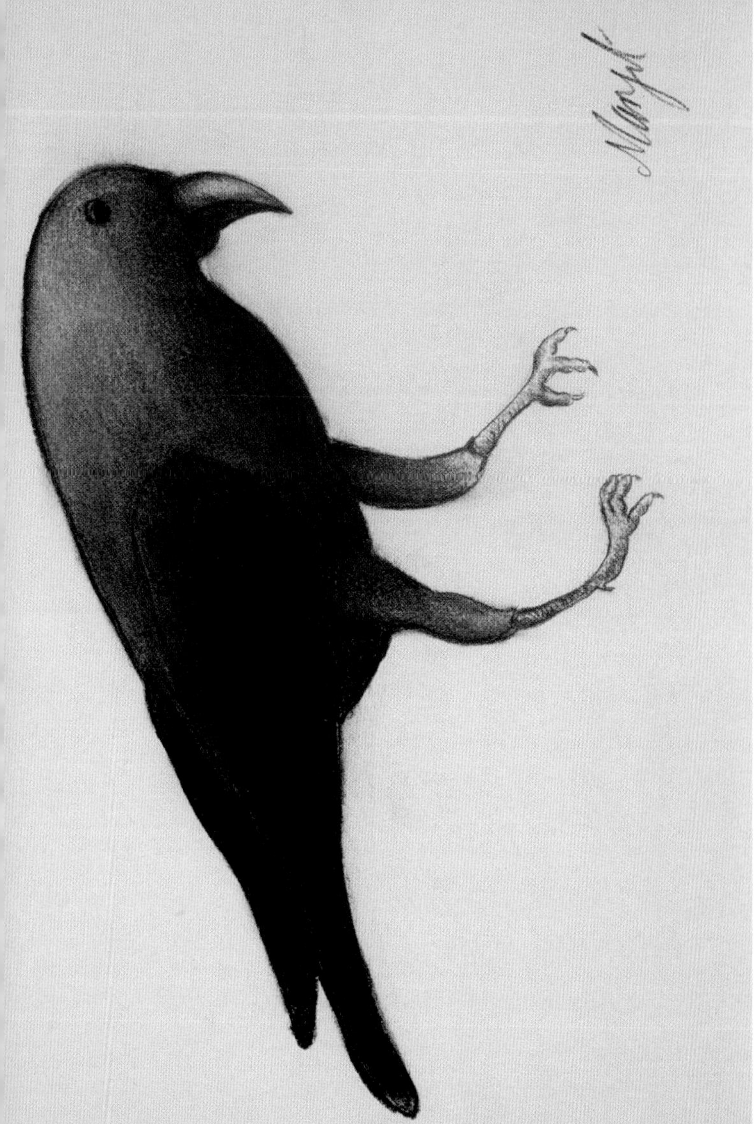

■ Drawing

Oil on canvas, 1999

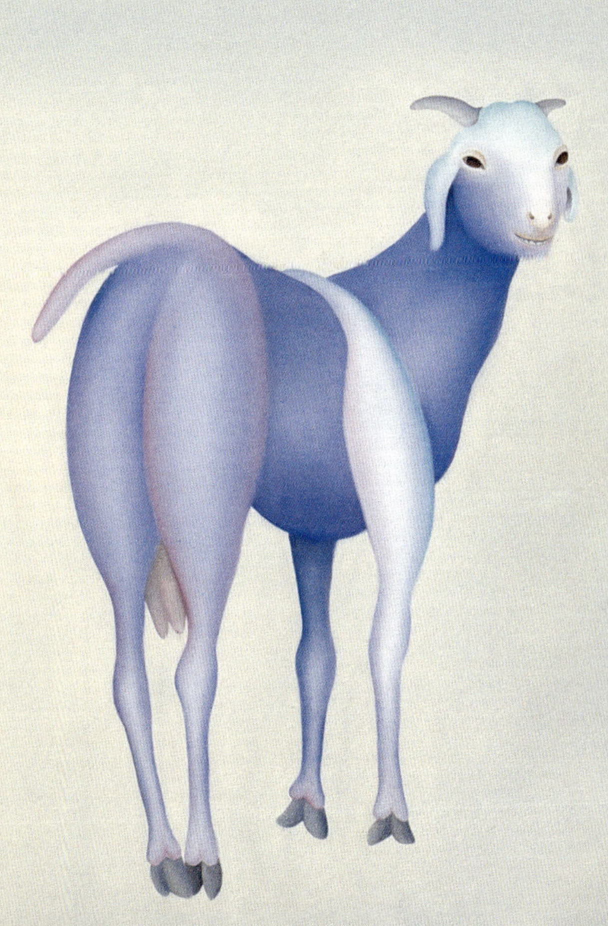

■ Goat

48" x 48", oil on canvas, 1995

■ *Front cover:* The solitary cowherd, *63" x 48", oil on canvas, 1994*